<u>Advance Praise for Worlds Apart</u>

[Worlds Apart] tells the captivating story of Marilyn Gardner's childhood as a 'third-culture kid', raised by her Christian, American missionary parents in the heart of Pakistan. Gardner's eloquent story of the trials, tribulations, and lessons of growing up as a bridge between these rich cultures serves as an important lens through which Americans and Pakistanis can learn more about one another and their important long-term partnership in a time when the gap between the two nations seems to be growing ever larger. By shedding light on how our faiths, our cultures, and our worlds are far more alike than different, Gardner's story is a must read for those wanting to build bridges.

~Ambassador Akbar Ahmed, Ibn Khaldun Chair of Islamic Studies,
American University, Washington, DC

[A] wonderful book, presenting in both a descriptive and reflective way the wonder of her childhood that took place in the mountains of northern Pakistan, the villages and deserts of southern Pakistan and the small towns of New England, along with some of the places in between.

As the only daughter in a remarkable family that included four brothers, Marilyn emerges as a sensitive observer with an impressive eye for detail as well as a developed memory for the small anecdote that often reveals a much larger meaning.

Part spiritual reflection, part childhood reminiscence and part travelogue, Marilyn's book will be especially welcomed by those trying to make sense of their own personal stories, especially if they involve transitions across multiple cultures and geographic locations.

A deeply moving observer of the places, people and events that have surrounded her, she demonstrates sensitivity and understanding toward an often misunderstood part of the world, presenting the sights, sounds, landscapes and peoples of Pakistan in ways that are largely absent in both newspaper headlines and superficial social media accounts that all too often know little and understand even less.

Americans growing up in Asia and Asians growing up in America will especially gravitate toward this account, capturing as it does the complexity as well as the wonder and astonishment of childhoods spent in unlikely places. It will also resonate strongly with missionary kids and third culture kids everywhere.

~ Ambassador Jonathan Addleton, author of The Dust of Kandahar *and* Some Far and Distant Place

It's been said that if you dig down into your story deep enough, you find the common things. I didn't grow up in Pakistan, and I didn't experience boarding school or life as a missionary kid. But that doesn't matter, because in this book Marilyn digs down deep enough into her own journey that I found myself resonating throughout. And crying.

The cross-cultural connections and the cross-cultural stretching, the faith struggles, the reverence of older missionaries, the questions about God's sovereignty in the midst of catastrophe, and the confusion surrounding the loaded word, Calling. It's all here.

We need this story. The missions community needs this story.

~Jonathan Trotter, International Pastoral Counselor and co-author of A-41: Essays on life and ministry abroad,

For anyone who has wrestled with heavy bouts of homesickness or lived through long stretches of loneliness, Marilyn Gardner's *[Worlds Apart]* is a gift.

For anyone who has walked through the valley of the shadow of death or of betrayal while simultaneously trying to hold onto faith in a good and loving God, this book is a light in your darkness.

For anyone who longs for the people and places of your past or has ever had to pack up a life and say goodbye, this book is a trustworthy traveling companion.